From Ashes to Hope

John Windell

Forward Movement
Cincinnati, Ohio

Morehouse Publishing
New York, Harrisburg, Denver

FORWARD MOVEMENT, an official, non-profit agency of the Episcopal church, is sustained through sales and tax-free contributions from our readers.

Copyright ©2011 Forward Movement
All rights reserved.

Cover design: Albonetti Design

Library of Congress Cataloging-in-Publication Data

Windell, John.
40 days of Lent : from ashes to hope / John Windell.
    p. cm.
ISBN 978-0-88028-328-1
1. Lent—Meditations. I. Title. II. Title: Forty days of Lent.
BV85.W477 2011
242'.34—dc23

2011022918

Printed in the United States of America

Morehouse Publishing
NEW YORK · HARRISBURG · DENVER

FORWARD MOVEMENT
412 Sycamore Street, Cincinnati, Ohio 45202-4195
800-543-1813   www.forwardmovement.org

Foreword

The Lenten season is intended as a time to focus on deepening our understanding of Christian living as we approach the joyous celebration of the resurrection of our Lord with special disciplines such as fasting, worship, service, and study. This volume was compiled not as a guide to those disciplines (though reference is made to them in some of these meditations), but as a series of short stories and vignettes about Christian discipleship in general. The author, John Windell, is a retired United Methodist pastor living in southern Indiana. He also serves as an overseas missionary in Tanzania, from which some of the stories that follow emanate. While some of his terminology differs from that commonly used in the Episcopal Church, Windell's passion for his Lord and for faithful living and his ability as a storyteller will make this collection a challenging and inspiring Lenten resource for any Christian, of any tradition.

—The Editors of Forward Movement

Preface

Many of the illustrating stories included with these Lenten reflections are from personal experiences. Others are from stories that I have read and documented, and still yet others are stories I have heard or read but cannot remember their sources.

I am thankful for all those who have written or told stories over the years that have impacted my life. Someone has indicated that story illustrations are like windows into truth. It is my prayer that these Lenten reflections greatly enrich your Lenten season.

—John E. Windell

Ash Wednesday

The black blob

*So we are ambassadors for Christ,
since God is making his appeal through us;
we entreat you on behalf of Christ, be reconciled to God.*

—2 Corinthians 5:20

Sometimes the cross turns into a black blob. When people come to the altar rail for the mark of ashes on Ash Wednesday, I try to make the marks resemble a cross. I make the sign of the cross on the forehead with my thumb, but sometimes it's just a black blob.

Why ashes? They are a sign of repentance, of sorrow and remorse for sins, of the elements from which we are composed and to which our bodies shall return. They are a way of getting in touch with our basic humanness. Ashes are messy. Sin is messy. The cross was messy. The flogging and the thorns were messy. Without confession and repentance, the messiness gets smeared all through us. A black blob is sometimes just the mark for us.

We cannot hide our identity; the ashes mark us. The universal Christian mark of baptism is not always a visible sign, but until we wipe the ashes off, our Ash Wednesday worship visibly marks us as Christian. Christians ought always to be visible ambassadors for Christ—acts of love, justice, and kindness should make us continually visible.

Sometimes we might be tempted to act out frustrations in a raucous manner—until we remember whose we are. Someone said the last thing he could remember his mother saying to him before departing home for an evening out was, "Remember whose you are." Not *who* you are, for that indicates an earthly family name. Remembering *whose* you are suggests a new perspective that begins in the mind of God.

How well do you wear the ashes?
Are you in a hurry to remove them?
What marks you as a Christian?

Holy God, as I begin this season of Lent, make me more conscious of your love for me. Show me ways to make my connection with you more visible. I pray through the name of Christ Jesus. Amen.

Thursday after Ash Wednesday

Brokenness and grace

*Create in me a clean heart, O God,
and renew a right spirit within me.*

—PSALM 51:11

Psalm 51 is the Bible's most searing expression of personal penitence, often thought to have been written by King David after the prophet Nathan had confronted him over his adultery with Bathsheba and his arranging the death of her husband Uriah (2 Samuel 11–12).

David, David, David! What have you done? What were you thinking? Sin grips us so easily, it seems. Satan knows the right times to tempt us. Sometimes we're on guard, but most of the time sin seems to sneak up on us. But not really—we know what we're doing and we know the consequences—but we do it anyway.

Does God still love us after we sin? How extensive is divine grace?

After we stumble and falter, we feel broken and useless. We feel broken when our lives do not turn out as we'd hoped and we know it is because of what we have done. Anxiety over things of which we are ashamed breaks our spirit. We feel worthless.

There is a remedy, a recourse for spiritual healing. Grace is unmerited favor. That's the simplest definition I know. It goes beyond comprehension. Augustine said, "God loves each of us as if there were only one of us." God's love is so exhaustive that nothing can separate us from it. This love of God is what we see in Christ Jesus our Lord.

When have you felt broken and useless?
How do you experience divine grace?

Gracious God, today I'm thankful that your love for me exceeds all boundaries. Forgive me for the brokenness that is in me and for the brokenness I have caused others. I pray this through the name of Christ Jesus. Amen.

Friday after Ash Wednesday

The old and the new

*Rend your hearts, and not your clothing.
Return to the LORD, your God, for he is gracious and
merciful, slow to anger, and abounding in steadfast love.*

—JOEL 2:13

When I was a teenager my grandparents' house burned to the ground. I watched it burn. It happened so quickly. It was devastating. No one could control the fire. The heat, the flames, my grandmother's cries, my grandfather's cracking voice. All this is forever etched in my mind.

The next day my grandparents stood in the burned-out house, just looking and remembering. A lifetime of memories. A family had grown up in that house. Now nothing was left. Just ashes. The things that wouldn't burn had melted.

My grandparents decided to rebuild. The next year a new home graced the farm landscape, on the location of the old house. But it wasn't the same house—it was better.

Lent is a time to remember the old and make room for the new. We remember the inadequacies and the incompleteness. We think about our imperfections and sin. We think about uncertainties and fears. We remember confession and repentance. We also remember that God has a plan for us that reaches beyond this earthly existence and beyond our comprehension.

Lent is a time when we say, "Here I am, God. Forgive my sin; mold and make me new according to your design."

How is God's new design on your life better than the old one? How is this changing you?

God, your presence is ever abounding. Teach me to acknowledge the newness you have for me today. I pray through the amazing name of Jesus. Amen.

Saturday after Ash Wednesday

Giving or grabbing?

...and your Father who sees in secret will reward you.
—Matthew 6:4b

Even in times of economic uncertainty, many of us live in the midst of abundance. Our culture still says, "Grab all you can with all the gusto you can muster!" How does that stack up against the Sermon on the Mount?

Some Christians today give as if they are impoverished. Some churches act as if they're impoverished, too, resorting to special fundraisers in an effort to get other people, even nonmembers, to support their ministries. It never works for long. Charles Paul Conn, in *Making It Happen: A Christian Looks at Money, Competition, and Success*, relates a story about "The Church of God Grill." A church started serving chicken dinners to help out with finances.

The dinners were so successful they cut out the church services altogether. The congregation's food was so good it forgot about the good news of Jesus. The church died because its food was so good.

The church is called to rescue people who are faltering. I once read that before we are invited to the marriage feast of the Lamb, we will be asked to present a letter of invitation from the poor. The faces of the poor are changing. Economic crisis has invaded places it has never been before. The church's calling is to respond to human need. As we bring our offerings and tithes to God, some important things will happen: the blessings of God will more than meet the needs of the poor, the church will be blessed because of obedience to God in Christ, and new disciples will be made.

During these days of Lent, examine your giving. We give in response to the ultimate gift. God gave Jesus for us and for our salvation.

How is my giving a testimony to my faith?
How has God blessed me and others through my giving?

Father God, I adore you. Help me to sense my abundance as your special gift to me. Teach me to share my blessings, that my giving will bring special joy to you. I pray through the name of my Savior, Jesus Christ. Amen.

First Sunday in Lent

A village without Christians

*Then you shall call, and the LORD will answer;
you shall cry for help, and he will say, Here I am.*
—ISAIAH 58:9

I was invited to join a mission trip to Ghana. The trip was scheduled to depart the United States the third week of September 2001. On September 11, terrorists attacked the United States and all subsequent flights were canceled. Our team prayed. We decided that if the flights were allowed, we would still proceed with the mission trip. Our flight was finally allowed and we traveled to Ghana.

The Ghanaians expressed deep sympathy for the U.S. and the victims of the attacks. Many asked what was so important about our message that we were willing to leave our country at a time like that.

The preaching was sometimes held in village churches. Toward the end of our trip, one of the pastors, Ibrahim Mohammed, asked me if I would preach in a village that had no Christians. The villagers had agreed that we could come. We arrived at the village, but only a few mothers and children met us. Pastor Ibrahim walked through the village inviting people to come to worship. At dusk a few more people arrived, perhaps fifty in all. Some Muslim men departed the village, passing directly by our worship area as a silent expression of their displeasure that Christians were worshiping in their village.

At the end of the preaching service, I extended the invitation to Christian discipleship. No one came forward. It was eerie. The people just sat and stared at us. Finally, Pastor Ibrahim led a closing prayer and we left the village. There were no handshakes, no well-wishing. It was a difficult moment.

Back home six months later, I received a letter from a person whose name I did not recognize. The man had been at the worship service in the village that had no Christians, and had quietly accepted God's offer of forgiveness through the sacrifice Jesus made on the cross. He couldn't openly admit that he had accepted Christ as his Savior for fear that he would have been ostracized from the village. However, since that time, in a period of six months, he had won ten others for Christ!

How is God equipping you to witness for Christ?
Have you led or could you introduce someone to Christ?

Heavenly Father, for the blessings of this day I give you thanks. I want to be an effective witness to your grace. Help me with the challenges and obstacles of becoming your witness. I pray through the name of Christ Jesus. Amen.

Monday, First Week of Lent

Covenants and promises

*I am establishing my covenant with you
and your descendants...*

—Genesis 9:9

A covenant is a formal agreement between two parties. The Bible tells of several covenants initiated by God with his people. God promises to be with us and to provide for us; we promise in response to live obediently. God is always faithful to these covenants, but we have not always been faithful. We intend to follow through, but our agendas become crowded.

The story is told of a man who, during the Great Depression, owned a sheep ranch in Texas. He lacked money to continue operating the ranch and was forced to live on government subsidies. Each day he worried about the mounting bills. Sometime later, a crew representing an oil company said there might be oil under his land. After a lease was signed, they set up their rig and drilled for oil.

A huge oil reserve was struck. Subsequent wells revealed even more oil. The rancher owned it all. He had been living on government relief but owned all that oil with its tremendous potential—yet for many years did not know it.

We usually do not know the blessings God has in store for us. Since creation, God has been making promises and preparations, inviting us to trust his promises. Regardless of the ways we've responded in prior times, God is faithful. We are asked to trust God with our life, our possessions, our families, and our future—to join in covenant with God. God's covenants say to us, "I love you."

What are the ways God is saying to you, "I love you"?
How are you in covenant with God?

Holy God, thank you for the covenant of unconditional love. Help me to be faithful to my promises to you. I offer this prayer through the name of Christ Jesus. Amen.

Tuesday, First Week of Lent

"People don't bite!"

*For your Name's sake, O LORD,
forgive my sin, for it is great.*
—PSALM 25:10

The words are still ringing in my ears, or perhaps I should say making tracks in my mind. The frustrated voice was that of the mother of three young children: "People don't bite! Animals bite—not people!" In her grocery cart, one child was wailing while the other two were looking at their mother with guilt etched on their faces.

We learn in stages, struggling again and again with the same temptations. We think we have learned the lesson, but then an unforeseen circumstance irritates us and we act out a frustration with an unacceptable gesture or unkind word—again.

Then we remember that we had promised not to respond to frustrations in that manner again. Like God's people throughout history, we break our covenant and then we must start over again, making peace with our loving and compassionate God and finding a grace-filled response—again.

God's love embraces us in spite of ourselves. Jesus offers grace, love, and forgiveness as if we had never sinned. Christ forgives us and renews us to begin our walk with him—again and again and again.

How is your spiritual growth taking place in stages?
How many times do you forgive others their trespasses against you?

Eternal and ever forgiving God, teach me again the lessons of forgiveness. Create in me the desire to be your child and to put my faith into practice. I pray through the name of Jesus, my Savior. Amen.

Wednesday, First Week of Lent

Mr. Gatlin

For Christ also suffered for sins once for all, the righteous for the unrighteous, in order to bring you to God.
—1 PETER 3:18

Mr. Gatlin was old and his eyes weak. He sold newspapers and candy in a little shop next to the post office. Every Sunday after church several young people would visit the shop and pick up a newspaper.

One day when Mr. Gatlin was not behind the counter one of the children pocketed a Snickers bar. She sneaked it home and walked as quietly as she could to her room to hide the candy bar under her pillow. At that very moment her mother appeared at the door of her room. Her mother asked her what she had stuffed under the pillow. Upon learning the truth, the mother hiked her daughter down to Mr. Gatlin's store.

"Mr. Gatlin," the young lady mumbled in embarrassment, "I took one of your candy bars." Her voice broke. She was afraid he would call the police or give her a tongue-lashing in front of the other customers. But he just looked at her.

"And you brought it back?" he asked.

"My mother made me," she confessed.

"Good. Now maybe you'd better sweep up around here and straighten out the pencils and notebooks," he said.

He handed her a stubby broom. She swept the floor, picked up candy and gum wrappers, and straightened items in the showcase. Then she replaced the broom and stood before him red-faced with embarrassment. He handed her the Snickers bar.

"Here, now it belongs to you," he said.

Thankfulness is an everyday occasion for Christians. God pours out so many abundant blessings on us. When

I am unloving, God loves me. When I am uncaring, God cares for me. When I am unkind, God is kind to me. When I am least deserving, God rescues me from the grasp of sin. For the selfless act of forgiveness on the cross I am thankful.

How has God's unconditional love been revealed to you? When did you receive an undeserved blessing?

Holy and loving God, thank you for the numerous acts of kindness you show me. Help me to reflect your kindness in my dealings with those who are unkind to me. I pray in the name of Jesus Christ, my Lord. Amen.

Thursday, First Week of Lent

Angels in Kentucky

He was in the wilderness forty days, tempted by Satan; and he was with the wild beasts; and the angels waited on him.

—MARK 1:13

My wife Karen and I always pray that God will watch over us on our travels.

We had been on a week's vacation to the Florida panhandle. While traveling through Kentucky back to Indiana, we decided we should trade for a better car before our next journey. I thought to myself that we would not tempt God again by making another trip in our old, run-down vehicle.

We stopped for our evening meal at one of those buffet restaurants that seem always to be located near interstate highways. When we returned to our car after our meal, I put the key in the ignition and all I heard was a clicking sound. I tried again, and nothing. It was late. Automobile dealers and garages were closed, and I had no idea where to find an auto supply store. Those were the days before cell phones. We were stuck. Suddenly what had been a routine trip had turned into a potential nightmare.

Through the parking lot came an older model, very used van. The driver leaned out of his window and asked if we were having problems. I explained our situation and asked if he could take me to an auto parts store to purchase a battery, which I supposed was the problem. He stopped and exited the van along with a couple of children. He said, "I have an extra battery here in the back of the van."

I thought to myself, *How many people carry an extra battery in their vehicle?* He unloaded the battery and brought along a toolbox as well. He began removing my battery and installing his extra one. Then he led me across town to an auto parts store that was open and where I purchased a new battery, which he installed for me, removing his old one. His kindness was extraordinary. I offered him money for his assistance but he would accept none. Prior to our leaving, we had a prayer of thanksgiving and praise together.

We had asked God to watch over our trip and provide care. God not only watched over us, but provided a family of angels to come to our rescue. I have never forgotten the evening that the angels ministered to us.

How have angels waited on you?
When have you been the angel in someone else's time of need?

Dear God, thank you for surrounding me with a holy presence. Today, teach me how to share your messages of love that I can be your representative in greater dimensions. I pray in the name of Jesus, my Savior. Amen.

Friday, First Week of Lent

The Great Stone Face

I am God Almighty; walk before me, and be blameless.
—GENESIS 17:1B

In the story of "The Great Stone Face" by Nathaniel Hawthorne, Ernest lived in a valley surrounded by great mountains. The rocks on the side of the mountains resembled a face. A legend said that one of the region's native sons would someday become a very noble man whose face would resemble the stone face on the mountainside. Ernest loved to look at the face. He spent hours gazing at it. As he grew up, he watched for someone who looked like it to return to the valley.

From time to time native sons returned. One had accumulated great wealth. Another had become a general. Yet another had become a well-known philosopher. Each time Ernest was disappointed that none resembled the Great Stone Face. Years later, when Ernest was an old man, a poet came. Surely he would be the one. As the poet heard Ernest talking he suddenly exclaimed, "Ernest is the image of the Great Stone Face!" And it was so. He had gazed at the face for so long it had become a part of him and now he resembled it.

This is true of Christians as well. Our goal is to resemble Jesus. As we spend time with God in prayer and practice our faith, we become extensions of God's love through Christ Jesus.

What place does God have in your daily schedule?
What helps you to grow more Christlike?

God my heavenly Father, help me today to walk with you. I invite you to be at home in my heart. I pray in the name of Jesus, my Savior. Amen.

Saturday, First Week of Lent

The birds

The poor shall eat and be satisfied, and those who seek the Lord shall praise him: "May your heart live for ever!"

—Psalm 22:25

This poem entitled "At the Winter Feeder," by John Leax, gives me hope for the struggles of these days. It helps me look beyond myself and see directly into the heart of God.

I pray it blesses you, too.

> His feather flame doused dull
> by icy cold,
> the cardinal hunched
> into the rough, green feeder
> but ate no seed.
> Through binoculars I saw
> festered and useless
> his beak, broken
> at the root.
> Then two, one blazing, one gray,
> rode the swirling weather
> into my vision
> and lighted at his side.
> Unhurried, as if possessing
> the patience of God,
> they cracked sunflowers
> and fed him
> beak to wounded beak
> choice meats.
> Each morning and afternoon
> the winter long,
> that odd triumvirate,
> that trinity of need,
> returned and ate
> their sacrament
> of broken seed.

"At the Winter Feeder," copyright ©1985 by John Leax. All rights reserved worldwide. Used by permission.

Have you heard the cry of the needy?
How are you responding?

Holy God, I need your insight. Help me to see Jesus more clearly in those who challenge me. I pray through the blessed name of Jesus. Amen.

Second Sunday of Lent

Meeting Mr. Jones

[Righteousness] will be reckoned to us who believe in him who raised Jesus our Lord from the dead, who was handed over to death for our trespasses and was raised for our justification.

—ROMANS 4:24-25

I once served two congregations in neighboring towns. The shortest route between them took me through an area known as "The Hollow." People in the Hollow did not return my waves as I passed by. I saw people carrying rifles and assumed they must be hunters. Many people sat on porches or walked idly along the road. They seemed unfriendly.

I learned that the people in the Hollow were descended from a family particularly unfriendly to outsiders and with a reputation for lawlessness. It was said they didn't pay their electric bills and climbed poles to reconnect when the utility company cut off their service. "There are shootings in the Hollow," someone told me. "Bodies are found and the law doesn't even investigate."

A certain Mr. Jones was said to run things in the Hollow, a terror of a man who drank a quart of whiskey a day and often shot people who crossed him. I started paying closer attention as I drove through the Hollow.

I eventually became acquainted with some of the folks in the Hollow. A few attended church now and then. One day I received a phone call asking me to visit a Mrs. Taylor in the Hollow. Her husband had just died. I had never entered a home in the Hollow before. I drove to the house and Mrs. Taylor invited me inside. We sat at her dining room table with a pot of coffee while she told me the story of her life. Her maiden name had been Jones, and she had lived in the Hollow her entire life.

The funeral began a long friendship with the family. Several members of the family began attending worship regularly. I met many of them—but never the notorious Mr. Jones.

One day I received a phone call from Mrs. Taylor. Mr. Jones wanted to talk with me but she wouldn't tell me why. I drove to her home again. She ushered me into her dining room and introduced me to her brother, Mr. Jones. He stood and shook my hand. He was tall and his face looked worn. His huge hand dwarfed mine. He offered me a cup of coffee and pulled a huge revolver from his belt and clanged it down on the table. I wanted to run away. Then he said, "I've asked the Lord to forgive me for my sins and he did. What do I do now?"

The next Sunday morning Mr. Jones stood at the altar of the church, made a public testimony to the saving power of Jesus Christ, and received the sacrament of baptism.

Through Mr. Jones, God taught me to love people regardless. We are all created in the image of God. Our spirits want freedom from guilt and assurance of acceptance from our Creator. Our spiritual completeness is found in the grace of God through Jesus Christ.

Whom do you find it most difficult to love?
How can you overcome this difficulty?

Holy God, thank you for those who have served as your mentors in my spiritual development. Help me today, to become a spiritual mentor for someone. I offer this prayer in the name of Jesus, my Savior. Amen.

Monday, Second Week of Lent

Forty-one imprisoned

*If any want to become my followers, let them deny themselves and take up their cross and follow me.
For those who want to save their life will lose it, and those who lose their life for my sake, and for the sake of the gospel, will save it.*

—Mark 8:34-35

Mission letters appealing for funds and asking for prayer regularly cross my desk. One such letter reported on a group of Christians imprisoned for their faith in a distant country. They were charged with insulting the dominant religion of the region. Through an ongoing appeal process, their sentences had been reduced from five years to three years and six months. As the appeals continued, mobs crowded into the courtrooms holding banners calling for the death penalty. Such demonstrations often result in stricter and longer sentences.

Later, I was able to visit them. One of the women prisoners told of how difficult it was to be separated from her three young children with her husband also in prison. But God had given her peace, she said: "God will look after them better than I can. I don't cry about them anymore." The children had been told that their parents were imprisoned not because they had done anything shameful and that they should be proud of their parents.

Another prisoner said, "We were allowed to spend quite some time with our friends, with two wardens listening to us. I was able to share the Word and some words of encouragement."

Forty-one Christians, all imprisoned for their faith. One looked almost like a child. He was just twenty-two. The oldest was seventy-two.

They volunteered to help the prison officials. Three helped with electricity problems and one taught English. The women planted a garden for which the wardens expressed appreciation. While we were there, one prisoner shared that he felt the Spirit of God was challenging him to go to the toughest place possible when he got out. He asked the whole group, "How many of you are willing to come with me?" All of them raised their hands.

These modern day prisoners for the gospel of Jesus put our Lenten preparations into perspective.

How would you respond to being imprisoned for your faith?
How can the gospel best be taken to places filled with violence and hatred?

God, I thank you for those who have denied self and carried the cross so that I could hear the story of salvation through Jesus. I pray for strength for those who are in prison for their faith today. I pray through the name of Jesus my Lord. Amen.

Tuesday, Second Week of Lent

Prayer meeting in Tanzania

Then a cloud overshadowed them, and from the cloud there came a voice, "This is my Son, the Beloved; listen to him!"

—MARK 9:7

Miracles are rare and extraordinary events. God uses them to get our attention and, through miracles, God receives glory, honor, and praise.

We were holding a seminar for pastors in Tanzania when we received a message from a young woman, which read, "Come and pray for me before I die."

I had met the young woman on a previous visit to the orphanage at Ilula. She had served on the staff and exemplified faith and generosity. She had left the staff position at the orphanage to attend college. During her first semester she became sick and was diagnosed as having suffered a stroke. She left school and returned home to get what little health care was available in rural Tanzania. She was on many church prayer lists in Africa, Europe, and North America. However, her condition only worsened.

Seven of us went to her home. We were ushered into the living room. The room was small. We filled the room. After we were seated, she entered. At first I didn't recognize her. She looked much older than her twenty-something years. She greeted each of us and told us about her condition and how the medicine had stopped working. She told us of several prayer groups that were interceding for her. After about fifteen minutes of sharing about her problems, we decided to gather around her, lay on hands, and pray for healing. As we were praying, the Spirit's presence overcame the young woman, who dropped to the floor and lay in a prostrate position. After what seemed about twenty minutes, the prayers came to a close. The young lady stood up in the midst of us and began flexing her arms and smiling.

Suddenly, the Spirit fell on one of the clergy in our group, who began to lead another concert of prayers. The young woman again fell to the floor and lay with her face on the floor uttering unintelligible sounds as we prayed. As the prayer time closed, she sat up, smiled, flexed her arms, and gave thanks to God.

The young woman later returned to college and is now a radiant testimony to the power of God to heal. We who gathererd in that prayer room and all who hear the story give God praise and glory.

Miracles are rare and extraordinary events. God uses them to get our attention. Through miracles, God receives glory, honor, and praise.

How have God's miracles been made evident to you?
How have you witnessed the miraculous bringing glory to God?

O Lord our God, how excellent is your name in all the universe. Thank you for visiting us with miracles. May our lives be living testimonies of your miraculous grace. I pray through the awesome name of Jesus. Amen.

Wednesday, Second Week of Lent

The lobster

*I the LORD your God…[show] steadfast love
to the thousandth generation of those who love me
and keep my commandments.*

—EXODUS 20:5-6

The growth of a lobster requires it to shed its shell at regular intervals. When its body begins to feel cramped inside the shell, the lobster instinctively looks for a safe spot to rest while the hard shell comes off, and the pink membrane inside forms the basis for the next shell.

Wherever the lobster goes to endure this process, it is very vulnerable. It can get tossed against a coral reef or eaten by a fish. A lobster must risk itself in order to grow.

God beckons us to new dimensions of spiritual awareness every day. As with the lobster, our spiritual shells can become too small, leaving us depressed, fearful, or angry. Sometimes we may be content to relax our spiritual training and become vulnerable to evil influences that infect us with sin. Seeking God's direction to strengthen our spiritual lives can make us vulnerable as well. Spiritual reflection, Bible study, and meditation stretch us. We learn new lessons that when applied increase our faith. Invariably, God calls us to depart from the familiarity of the comfortable levels to which we've grown accustomed and to follow the direction of love into new areas of mission and service.

By expanding our spiritual dimensions we remain on the cutting edge of mission and service for Christ Jesus.

Where is God challenging you to be vulnerable?
How do you measure spiritual growth?

O Holy God, thank you for revealing your grace to me in Jesus. Expand my spiritual dimensions that I may be your servant in greater ways. I pray in the name of my Savior, Jesus. Amen.

Thursday, Second Week of Lent

A silly football game

*Serve the LORD your God with all your heart
and with all your soul.*

—Deuteronomy 10:12

Lent is for remembering who we are in relation to God. Lent is for self-examination as we ponder again the message of the cross and prepare ourselves for the victory of Easter.

I remember a silly story about a group of animals in the jungle who decided to have a football game. The problem was that no one could tackle the rhinoceros. When he received the opening kick-off, he rambled for a touchdown. He was unstoppable.

The score was seven to nothing immediately. Somehow, the other team managed to keep the ball away from the rhino the remainder of the first quarter. At the beginning of the second quarter, they tied the score seven to seven.

The lion warned the zebra on the kick-off not to kick it to the rhinoceros, but the zebra ignored the warning. The rhino caught the ball and there he was racing for the touchdown. Suddenly, out of nowhere, a vicious tackle brought him down. When the animals got up, they discovered that a centipede had made the tackle.

"That was fantastic!" congratulated the lion. "But where were you on the opening kick-off?"

The centipede replied, "I was still putting on my shoes."

Are we like the centipede who took the time to prepare himself before beginning his work? Or do we rush into things with no forethought or preparation? God is calling us to be involved in faith's game of life and love, to be prepared to celebrate the victory. Lent is a time to make certain we're ready for the game.

Are you still putting on holy shoes?
What spiritual preparations are you making to tackle evil?

Eternal God, thank you for the gift of life. Help me to seek ways to be prepared and ready for service. I pray through the name of Jesus, my Savior. Amen.

Friday, Second Week of Lent

Twenty-five students

For the message about the cross is foolishness to those who are perishing, but to us who are being saved it is the power of God.
—1 Corinthians 1:18

Many people are just waiting for someone to tell them about Jesus, but don't exactly know what they are waiting for. They know their spiritual lives are incomplete. They sense a vacuum where faith belongs, but questions of faith and eternity make them nervous. To offset these feelings of incompleteness they fill their lives with more work, more time-consuming events, and more possessions, all intended to generate feelings of contentment and happiness.

One of the mission letters that comes across my desk is the *Campus Crusade for Christ International* newsletter. The March 2008 edition reported that twenty-five students decided to enter into a personal relationship with Jesus Christ, at a "Freshman Survival Kit" table at the University of Maryland. Twenty-five young people decided to become Christians when they heard the Good News of Jesus. This did not occur in some remote pagan territory as we might expect; it happened in mainstream United States, where God's name is even on the money!

Many people today have no idea what Christians believe. Their only instruction booklet on Christianity consists of the actions and responses to situations that they observe in their church-going neighbors.

Oftentimes this instruction is less than perfect. A witness for Christ Jesus requires some preparation. As we pray for God to use us as instruments of the Good News, some amazing things happen. First, we find ourselves asking faith questions or joining a Bible study group to learn more about Jesus. Then we increasingly discover that God is placing us in situations to answer the faith questions people are asking. Third, people begin to feel comfortable discussing faith and sharing the Good News of Jesus with us. Eventually, we acquire the desire to lead someone to Jesus Christ. Finally, God places us in a particular situation and we choose to seize the opportunity and pray with someone to receive Jesus.

In these weeks of Lenten preparation, pray for God to use you to bring someone to Christ.

Have you led anyone to become a Christian?
How can you prepare to lead someone to Christ?

Dear God, today I thank you for the gift of salvation. I pray for an increased faith to win someone to Christ Jesus today. I pray in the name of Jesus. Amen.

Saturday, Second Week of Lent

Faith and youth

His disciples remembered that he had said this; and they believed the scripture and the word that Jesus had spoken.

—John 2:22

Brooks Adams kept a diary from his boyhood. One special day when he was eight years old he wrote in his diary, "Went fishing with my father, the most glorious day of my life." Throughout the next forty years, he never forgot that day. He made repeated references to it in his diary, commenting on the influence that day had on his life.

Brooks's father was an important man; he was Charles Francis Adams, the United States Ambassador to Great Britain under the Lincoln administration. He too made a note in his diary about the fishing trip. "Went fishing with my son; a day wasted." Yet it was not a waste. It was probably the best investment of time he ever made.

I read about a man who sold square watermelons. They were novelties. People were buying them up as fast as he could grow them. He had placed a cubed-shaped box around each melon as it was growing. I am reminded of how easily growing things can be shaped.

Studies have concluded that many of the problems of adolescence are caused by a lack of love and parental guidance in the home. Parents are often so immersed in work and hobbies that quality time with their children is nonexistent. Some never take time to learn the likes and dislikes of their children. Few parents can remember the last time they spent a whole day devoted entirely to their children.

As parents, grandparents, teachers, and Christians, we are models for Christ. Growing minds watch and take note. All living things are growing—and growing things are still being shaped. Make plans to spend some quality time with a young family member.

How can I be more present to love and guide my family members?
How can I best relate my faith in Christ to a young person in my family?

Dear Heavenly Father, I thank you for the ways others have influenced me to remember your acts of love and kindness. Today, help me to model your teachings through all my words and actions. I offer my prayer in the name of Jesus. Amen.

Third Sunday of Lent

The lady and the devil

Go home to your friends,
and tell them how much the Lord has done for you,
and what mercy he has shown you.

—Mark 5:19

The person on the other end of the line sounded desperate: "There's a lady here threatening to commit suicide. Can you come?" I jotted the directions and whispered a prayer for the woman. When I arrived, a man was standing at the door waving for me to come in.

Sitting in the middle of the floor, a bottle of pills in one hand and a beer in the other, with hair disarrayed, shouting obscenities, sat a young woman. She shouted, "I'm going to kill myself today and you're going to watch, preacher! Ha! Ha! Ha!"

I prayed for direction and asked her whether she wanted to get well. "A part of me does," she said. I spoke to the part of her that wanted to get well and prayed for the evil spirit to depart, in the name of Jesus. She calmed down. I explained the love of Christ Jesus to her and told her that the evil spirit was gone.

I asked her if she had a Bible. She ran across the room and brought me a Bible filled with newspaper clippings and memorabilia. Together we read the scriptures about the evil that had been in her and the peace she now felt. She confessed her sins and invited Jesus to be her Savior.

The next day she visited my office. I learned that she had three children who were living with their father. After having become addicted to drugs, she had been dismissed from her job as a nurse for stealing drugs.

She began to attend a Bible study group and church worship services. She gave her witness for Christ at Sunday morning worship services and shared her testimony of faith at a revival service. But the addiction was strong, and after several failures she was admitted to a treatment facility. She completed treatment, and then continued witnessing for the saving power of Christ Jesus.

Like the Gerasene demoniac in Mark 5, she told her story to those who had known about her bouts and her struggles with addiction. They too were amazed and praised God.

How is your witness to Christ stronger than evil?
Where have you seen evil defeated through Christ Jesus?

Heavenly Father, I thank you for delivering me from the grip of the evil one. Help me today to witness to your saving grace. I pray through the wonderful name of Jesus, my Savior. Amen.

Monday, Third Week of Lent

The boy and the alligator

*Let all those whom the LORD has redeemed
proclaim that he redeemed them
from the hand of the foe.*

—PSALM 107:2

A Florida boy decided to go for a swim in the lake behind his house. He dove in, not realizing that an alligator was swimming toward him.

While working in the yard, his father saw the two as they swam closer. He ran to the lake yelling for his son to come back. Hearing the fear in his voice, the boy made a U-turn and swam toward the shore as quickly as he could.

Both the father and the alligator caught the boy just as he reached the dock where his father was standing. The father held his son by the arms as the alligator grabbed the boy's legs. A neighbor heard the commotion, retrieved a rifle, and shot the alligator.

A reporter interviewed the boy during his hospital stay and commented on the deep wounds left on the boy's legs by the alligator's teeth. With obvious pride, the boy said, "Look at my arms. I have wounds on them, too. I have them because my dad's fingernails wouldn't let go."

We too have wounds and scars. Perhaps not from the vicious bite of a wild animal, but the wounds and scars of sin from times past. Some of those scars were caused by our foolish decisions and give us deep regret. But some are there because God wouldn't let go of us.

When did God hold onto you when you were nearly lost?

Holy and loving God, thank you for the depth of your love for me. I pray that your saving love will be at home in me today. I pray in the blessed name of Jesus. Amen.

Tuesday, Third Week of Lent

The dolly and hot water bottle

Before they call I will answer.
—Isaiah 65:24

This story came to me through e-mail, from a friend:

One night I had worked hard to help a mother in the labor ward, but in spite of all we could do, she died, leaving us with a tiny premature baby and a crying two-year-old daughter. We would have difficulty keeping the baby alive because we had no incubator. A student midwife went to stoke up the fire and fill a hot water bottle, but rushed back in distress to tell me that the bottle had burst. Our last hot water bottle. In Central Africa, where our mission is, these bottles do not grow on trees, and there are no drugstores down forest pathways. The midwife slept with the baby near the fire.

The following noon I went to daily prayers with the children in the orphanage. I explained our problem with the hot water bottle, and that the baby could so easily die if she got chilled. I also told them of the two-year-old sister, crying because her mother had died.

One ten-year-old girl, Ruth, prayed with the usual blunt conciseness of our African children, "Please God, send us a water bottle. It'll be no good tomorrow, as the baby will be dead. Please send the bottle this afternoon." She added, "And would you please send a dolly for the little girl so she'll know you really love her?"

Could I honestly say "Amen" to that? Oh, yes, I know that God can do everything. But there are limits, aren't there? The only way God could answer this prayer would be by sending me a parcel from home, and in four years I had never received one. And who would send a hot water bottle? I lived on the equator!

That afternoon when I reached home, there, on the veranda, was a large parcel, from my former Sunday school class. The orphanage children watched as I lifted out brightly colored jerseys for them and knitted bandages for the leprosy patients. Then, in the bottom of the box I felt—could it be? Yes! A brand-new, rubber hot water bottle. I cried. I had not actually believed that God would do this.

Ruth rushed forward, crying out, "If God has sent the bottle, he must have sent the dolly, too!" Rummaging down to the very bottom of the box, she pulled out a small, beautifully dressed dolly. Her eyes shown. She had never doubted.

That parcel had been on the way for five whole months. The class leader had heard and obeyed God's prompting to send a hot water bottle, even to the equator, and one of the girls had put in a dolly for an African child—five months before, in answer to the believing prayer of a ten-year-old to bring it "that afternoon."

When has God startled you with an answer to prayer? If never, could you be praying too timidly?

Dear God, I thank you for the prayers of children to teach us lessons about faith. Let my prayer life be as real today as Ruth's. I pray through the name of Jesus. Amen.

Wednesday, Third Week of Lent

Worldwide missions

You shall love the Lord your God with all your heart, and with all your soul, and with all your mind, and with all your strength. The second is this, you shall love your neighbor as yourself. There is no other commandment greater than these.
—MARK 12:29-31

Some ask why I participate in so many mission projects. Perhaps the following story from somewhere will help.

It started with a crude little leaflet that told a touching story about a missionary effort in Africa. At the end there was an appeal for assistance. As I tossed the leaflet into the wastebasket, I wondered where they got my name and address. Why would anyone presume that I would be interested in a mission in a place I had never heard of?

Finished sorting the mail, I turned to a favorite magazine. An article about disasters in America caught my attention. Because of a hurricane, a flood, or a tornado, people in prosperous middle America had been left absolutely destitute. People from all over the world had sent food, clothing, and assistance. I was especially impressed by a generous food package from a congregation in China. An American missionary had told a Chinese congregation about the need in the United States and asked for prayers. In the midst of their own need, this Chinese congregation took their concern beyond prayers. The writer explained that the Chinese believe that all people under heaven are one family.

I went fishing in the wastebasket for that leaflet from Africa.

Our Lenten examination of Christ Jesus compels us toward new and stronger relationships with others:

I sought my soul, but my soul I could not see.
I sought my God, but my God eluded me.
I sought my brother, and I found all three.
—WILLIAM BLAKE

How have you found God in others?
How have mission projects influenced your faith?

Heavenly Father, thank you for providing so abundantly for me. Give me a burden to share my abundance with those who have so little. I pray through the name of Jesus. Amen.

Thursday, Third Week of Lent

"We are the church"

*We are what God has made us,
created in Christ Jesus for good works,
which God prepared beforehand to be our way of life.*

—EPHESIANS 2:10

"I am the church. You are the church. We are the church together!" We sing this song with much gusto, celebration, praise, and thanksgiving. As the church, we are responsible for loving all Christians. God gives us the people in our local congregation to practice on.

Sometimes God tests us by putting us in congregations with people we can't stand. If we can love these people, we can love anyone! Some people are just like us and therefore easy to love. But some people with whom we worship and pray are so different from us. God gives us some very difficult people to practice on. Still, we are the body of Christ, joined as sisters and brothers in this family of God.

These spiritual siblings of ours feel differently about some aspects of our faith. Some interpret the Bible differently. Some believe in a different form of baptism. Some will vote against our candidates in the next election.

Sunday after Sunday we overcome the differences, join together in heart and hand, and pray our most sincere prayers for each other. We seek to become children of God and to know God's will. As disciples of Christ Jesus we model ourselves after him, seeking to become like him as we offer ourselves as servants to the whole world.

> *I am the church. You are the church.*
> *We are the church together!*
> *All who follow Jesus, all around the world!*
> *Yes, we're the church together.*

How can you express love to those whose beliefs differ from yours? How can we share faith with those who have caused us harm?

Lord God, today I thank you for the church. I pray that I will be more sensitive to the ways you are stretching me to love others. I offer this prayer in the name of Jesus. Amen.

Friday, Third Week of Lent

Rain

> *For everything there is a season,*
> *and a time for every matter under heaven.*
> —ECCLESIASTES 3:1

She had been shopping with her mom in Wal-Mart. She appeared to be six years old, this beautiful red-haired, freckle-faced image of innocence. It was pouring outside, the kind of rain that gushes over the top of gutters, in such a hurry to hit the earth it has no time to flow down the spout. We all stood there under the awning and just inside the door of the Wal-Mart. Some of us waited patiently for the rain to let up, while others were irritated because nature had messed up their hurried day.

The child's voice was sweet as it broke the hypnotic trance we were all caught in. "Mom, let's run through the rain," she said.

"No, honey. We'll wait until it slows down a bit," Mom replied.

The child waited another minute and repeated, "Mom, let's run through the rain."

"We'll get soaked if we do," Mom said.

"No, we won't. Remember what you said this morning?" the young girl asked as she tugged her Mom's arm. "When you were talking to Daddy about his cancer, you said, 'If God can get us through this, he can get us through anything!'"

Everyone stopped dead silent. No one knew what the mother would say. Would she laugh it off and scold her daughter for being silly? Would she ignore her? Or did she realize this was a moment of affirmation in a young life, a time when innocent trust can be nurtured so that it will bloom into faith?

"Honey, you are absolutely right. Let's run through the rain. If God lets us get wet, well, maybe we just needed washing," the mother said. Then off they ran. We all stood watching, smiling and laughing as they darted past cars and through puddles. They got soaked. They were followed by a few others who screamed and laughed like children all the way to their cars.

And yes, I ran. I got wet. I needed washing.

You can lose your possessions, your money, your health, but no one can take away your precious memories. Take time and the opportunities to make memories every day.

"For everything there is a season, and a time for every matter under heaven." I hope you still take time to run through the rain.

When was the last time a child helped you with the reality of faith?

God, thank you for the joyful expressions in living. Today help me to have a refreshing time with your plans for me. Teach me more about your joy. I pray in the name of Jesus. Amen.

Saturday, Third Week of Lent

Turn your bowl upside down

*Give, and it will be given to you.
A good measure, pressed down, shaken together,
running over, will be put into your lap;
for the measure you give will be the measure you get back.*

—LUKE 6:38

A beggar in India held out his bowl by the side of the road. Passers-by would drop a few grains of rice into it. Occasionally, someone dropped a coin into his hand.

One day he saw a large procession coming down the road. "This is good," he thought. "It looks like a prince is coming. Surely he will give me a gold coin today."

It was indeed a prince, and he stopped beside the beggar, who held out his bowl and waited eagerly to see what this man of royalty would drop into it.

To his surprise the prince asked, "Will you please give me your rice?"

"I can't do that; it is all I have," the beggar answered.

Again the prince said, "I want your rice."

"No, I can't give you my rice. It's all I have to eat," was the firm reply.

The prince made a third request for the rice. Slowly the beggar took three grains of rice out of his bowl and put them into the hand of the prince, who then reached into a bag hanging at his belt and took out three nuggets of gold, which he dropped into the bowl. As the beggar looked at them he thought regretfully, "Oh, why didn't I turn my bowl upside down in his hand?"

Jesus once commented about a poor widow's act of giving. Her two pennies amounted to more than all the other gifts because had she turned her bowl upside down for God (Luke 21:1-4).

Whenever we turn our bowls upside down for Christ Jesus, amazing things take place. We are given a good measure in return. It is packed down, shaken together, and it spills over into our laps.

When was the last time you gave yourself completely to God?
How does God return the blessings to you in good measure?

Our Loving God, thank you for providing so abundantly for me. Guide my spiritual growth, that my giving is acceptable to you. I pray in the name of Jesus, my Lord and Savior. Amen.

Fourth Sunday of Lent

A Congolese mother

For you always have the poor with you, and you can show kindness to them whenever you wish; but you will not always have me.

—MARK 14:7

When I visited the Congo a few years ago, a mother asked me, through an interpreter, if my children get enough to eat. I assured her that my family is well cared for, with an abundance of food to eat. I then asked about her family. I'll never forget the pain on her face when she said, "We plan to eat one meal a day, and three days of the week we do not eat." How can those who live in the midst of abundance respond to that?

When the media brings us news stories and photos of people facing immediate suffering, the world community acts swiftly to alleviate the crisis. However, when the cameras fade away to some other story, the sad faces of the suffering recede from the public eye and their problems begin to escalate. Documentaries rarely show us the faces of the estimated forty million people around the world who die from hunger, unclean water, or malnutrition-related illnesses each year.

The suffering of others, whether nearby or on the other side of the globe, can seem overwhelming—the poor are always with us. We cannot cure every ill, right every wrong, or solve every problem. We must leave much of that work to God. But while we cannot make the world perfect, we can make the world better. We cannot do everything for everybody, but we can do something for somebody. And we give glory to God when we care for the poor.

How and for whom are you making the world better today?

Holy God, I praise and thank you for providing countless blessings for me. Challenge me to give to the poor. I pray in the name of Jesus. Amen.

Monday, Fourth Week of Lent

Faith break

*Show me your ways, O Lord,
and teach me your paths.*

—Psalm 25:3

Carol Gathagan told this story in one of her *Faith Break* broadcasts.

A few years ago, a couple of Colorado youngsters, a brother and a sister ages six and seven, watched a TV report about the plight of Rwandan refugees. They wanted to help. They decided to set up a lemonade stand at the curb, with the profits to go to help the refugees. Backed by their mother and some free promotion from a radio station, they earned $1,000 for their cause.

Down the street about five blocks, a couple of brothers, ages seven and eight, broke into their school and vandalized two classrooms before school security people caught them. Their brief rampage cost taxpayers more than $20,000.

The father of the vandals told the juvenile judge, "You can't teach kids what's right and wrong anymore. They watch television all the time and pick up their values from the tube."

The mother of the youngsters who raised money for the refugees told a reporter, "We've always tried to teach our children that there are needy people in the world, and we should do all we can to help them."

Who are some people over whom you have influence?
What are they learning from you?

Eternal God, give me the grace to teach by example. Teach me to follow your direction in my life. I pray through the name of Christ Jesus. Amen.

Tuesday, Fourth Week of Lent

Café 458

*How precious is your steadfast love, O God!
All people may take refuge in the shadow of your wings.*

—Psalm 36:7

A place of refuge can also be a place of respect. In his book *Living Faith*, Jimmy Carter writes about Café 458 in Atlanta, where homeless people get a hug and a warm welcome, then sit down at a table, choose the food they want, and order it from a waiter.

A. B. Short, a salesman, and his wife, Ann Conner, a nurse practitioner, founded Café 458 in 1988, recognizing that people who need both a good meal and help do not benefit from standing hours a day in soup kitchen lines. At Café 458, the "guests" make reservations for a month at a time and will be given extensions if they are making progress toward improving their lives. The volunteers who run Café 458 live next door. They get to know the guests well, referring those with serious problems, such as addiction to drugs or alcohol, to treatment centers, and working directly with others.

Roy had slept in a dumpster for ten years before being welcomed to Café 458. Treated with care and respect, he stopped selling cocaine, got a job with a landscaper, made foreman in six months, and began to believe in God. Roy found a new life.

Hundreds of people have passed through Café 458, regaining their dignity as human beings in the process. Many now give back by helping as volunteers. Of those who have gone through the drug rehabilitation program, only 8 percent have relapsed. Steadfast love is precious and powerful.

How are you helping the homeless or the hungry in your community?

O Lord God, bless those who give of themselves as volunteers in charitable programs and agencies. Show me how I can serve as your representative in my community. I ask this in Jesus' name. Amen.

Wednesday, Fourth Week of Lent

Kayla's tooth

One thing have I asked of the LORD;
one thing I seek;
that I may dwell in the house of the LORD
all the days of my life;
to behold the fair beauty of the LORD
and to seek him in his temple.

—PSALM 27:5

The phone rang in the middle of the night. Our six-year-old granddaughter, Kayla Dawn, called out to me "Papaw, I lost my tooth!" It was her first, and she had to tell us. It couldn't wait until tomorrow.

Sometimes things just cannot wait. If we put off Lenten disciplines, Easter will slip up on us and we'll be unprepared for the greatest miracle ever.

To behold the beauty of God is to be totally immersed in the teaching and mission of Christ Jesus. Living in the Lord's presence may mean removing some clutter from our lives in order for the messages of Christ to find space to grow and flourish. A prayer assessment of our lives may reveal habits that limit the blessings of God from reaching us. Confession and repentance may reveal that a spiritual housecleaning is needed. A trip to the resale shop with those items in our lives that are no longer useful might be the order of the day. Just as we give away clothing that no longer fits, we may need to exchange some of our perspectives and attitudes.

Kayla's baby tooth had outgrown its usefulness. A new and better tooth was being formed. In order to keep up with her body's demands, the baby tooth had to give way to the new. Our bodies get rid of the old to bring on the new and better. It works that way in our spiritual lives also. To live in the presence of God is to continually re-evaluate the old and make a place for the new. Don't wait; do it now.

Have you made a spiritual house cleaning recently?
Have you experienced the joy that comes with renewal?

Thank you, God, for the gift of life in all its splendor. Help me today to get rid of the old self and prepare for your new blessing in my life. I pray through the name of Jesus. Amen.

Thursday, Fourth Week of Lent

The day the road widened

*On this day the LORD has acted;
we will rejoice and be glad in it.*

—PSALM 118:24

Traces of tears were still visible on our faces. We had just finished saying our good-byes to some of the world's most loving, compassionate, and impoverished people. Our mission team had left its two-week, makeshift home at the Ilula Orphanage and was traveling by charter bus to Mikumi National Park near Morogoro, Tanzania.

We were the best kind of tired. The team had put into place a new drainage system, removed an old unused building, repaired sewing machines, worked in the storeroom, built a rabbit hutch, put a gasoline engine on a wringer washing machine, taught basic health care, practiced dentistry, visited foster families, met with teachers, assisted with tractor maintenance, taught a pastors' seminar, painted, varnished, and generally fixed up. The singing and witnessing of the orphans had spiritually energized us. The best kind of tired is physical exhaustion accompanied by joy. It comes from giving of ourselves for the least of God's children.

The charter bus was passing a slow vehicle when a rapidly approaching truck appeared from the opposite direction. The winding narrow mountain road was barely wide enough for two vehicles, let alone three. A collision seemed certain. We braced for the crash. Somehow, God widened the road that day and three vehicles passed each other without a scratch. Someone shouted, "Mungu ni mwema!" (God is good!)

Everyone on the bus exclaimed in unison, "Amen!"

God is attempting to get our attention. God is continually rescuing us. God wants to increase our faith. However, God needs our permission.

How has God rescued you?
Have you told anyone?

My loving Father, thank you for all the times you've been my protection. Guide me today to share the stories of your watch over me. I pray through the name of Jesus, my Lord. Amen.

Friday, Fourth Week of Lent

Carl and trust relations

*But be doers of the word,
and not merely hearers who deceive themselves.*

—JAMES 1:22

Carl taught me some valuable lessons. He was in his seventies, a carpenter, almost always smoking a cigarette and drinking coffee. Carl taught me about alcoholism and life in the midst of a caring community. He had no college degree, no list of accomplishments, but a wisdom that originated from beyond himself.

Carl taught me about Alcoholics Anonymous. The members of AA have a two-sided solution to life's problems. First, they turn everything over to God, whom they refer to as the Higher Power. Secondly, they ask others for help. It's hard enough to turn things over to God, but asking for help can be even harder. Carl and his friends at AA had learned the secret of being a caring community. By risking themselves and exposing their weaknesses, they developed trusting relationships. These kinds of relationships build genuine community.

Evangelism has been defined as one starving brother telling another where to find bread. We are at best weaklings, risking ourselves to help the weak. We all need help, and we all provide help.

At mission sites in developing nations, I witnessed the weak helping the weak. I saw people risking their lives to help one another. I saw people at worship, faces aglow with a holy presence, singing and dancing to the beat of a drum. A genuine spirit of Christ surrounds the church in emerging countries, as they become doers of the word and not merely hearers.

The lessons Carl taught me are still making a difference in my life. My life is enriched as I turn to God and seek the help of others. Trusting relationships are natural results in a caring community. We are called to become caring communities of faith.

Who has been instrumental in teaching you about the caring community of faith?
To whom have you been the teacher?

My heavenly Father, thank you for all those who have taught me the valuable lesson of caring. Help me to teach the lessons of love and care to others today. I pray in the name of Jesus. Amen.

Saturday, Fourth Week of Lent

Winsome missionary

*And whatever you do, in word or deed,
do everything in the name of the Lord Jesus,
giving thanks to God the Father through him.*

—COLOSSIANS 3:17

A missionary visited one of the islands of the South Pacific. When he told the people about Jesus, one of them remarked, "Oh, he used to live here." The missionary, surprised, inquired about the meaning of the statement. He learned that a few years earlier, another missionary had spent some time in the area. Although he hadn't known their language, he had helped them in every possible way, and his life radiated the presence of Christ. Now as the islanders heard about Jesus, they concluded that he must have been the kind friend who had visited them a few years earlier.

It has been said, "To win some we must be winsome." As we clothe ourselves with Christ, we become conformed to the image of God. The love of God binds everything together in perfect harmony and becomes an appealing force impacting the lives of those around us.

I read somewhere, "A Christian is one who makes it easier for other people to believe in God."

I had planned a beautiful modern home, but the voice of God came to me through a Burundi man who said, "I have no home."

I dreamed of a second house in the country for relaxing on the weekends, but the voice of God came to me through a refugee who said, "I have no country."

I decided that I needed a new kitchen, but the voice of God came to me through a child from the Congo who said, "I have no cup."

I started to purchase a computerized washer and dryer, but the voice of God came to me from a mother in Darfur who said, "My children have no clothes."

How have others represented Christ to you?
How are you representing Christ to others?

O Holy God, today I thank you for providing for me. My prayer today is for you to show me how I can help those who lack basic necessities of living. I pray through the name of Christ Jesus. Amen.

Fifth Sunday of Lent

Coffee cup

For we do not proclaim ourselves; we proclaim Jesus Christ as Lord and ourselves as your slaves for Jesus' sake.
—2 Corinthians 4:5

I generally have a cup of coffee in my hand, on my desk, or in close proximity. A coffee cup is a vessel that holds liquid that can be poured out. But when my cup is empty, though it does not serve as a coffee cup, it can still be useful. It can be a container for small objects or a knickknack on a shelf. But if I want to use it for its intended purpose, I must return to the coffee pot for a refill.

The church is like a cup filled with God's love and grace. When it is full, its purpose is to be emptied. It is to be poured out for a needy, sick, hungry, hurting, thirsty world. The church's purpose is to be emptied.

And then the church needs a refill. When the church has emptied itself but is not getting a refill of God's grace, it's useless as a church, though it may still be a landmark, a street identifier, a meeting place for social gatherings, or the site of community fundraisers.

When the church is emptied out and its members lift their hearts to God for a refill, God fills it up again. The church fills up, runs over the brim, and splashes out. Everyone who gets touched by the overflow receives extraordinary blessings. The church gives as it receives. Its purpose is to receive, so that it can pour out.

Has God filled your cup?
What extraordinary blessings are being poured out from your church?

Holy God, thank you for the church. I pray that you will use me to be a blessing today. I pray through the name of Jesus. Amen.

Monday, Fifth Week of Lent

It comes with the ticket

I came that they may have life, and have it abundantly.
—John 10:10b

A poor European family saved for years to buy tickets to sail to America. Once at sea, they carefully rationed the cheese and bread they had brought for the journey. After three days the boy complained to his father, "I hate cheese sandwiches. If I don't eat anything but cheese sandwiches before we get to America, I'm going to die." Giving the boy his last nickel, the father told him to go to the ship's galley and buy an ice cream cone.

When the boy returned a long time later with a wide smile, his worried dad asked, "Where were you?"

"In the galley eating three ice cream cones and a steak dinner!"

"All that for a nickel?" asked the father.

"Oh no, the food is free," the boy replied. "It comes with the ticket."

In these days we are confronted by a hurting world scarred by homelessness, hunger, malnutrition, contaminated water, injustice, oppression, disease, strife, and war. Our mission involvement comes in response to the one who said, "As you did to one of the least of these…you did it to me" (Matthew 25:40).

Redemption not only promises eternal life, but, like the ticket, provides for our needs while we serve as Christ's ambassadors on the journey. Christians are called to share their abundance in order that others may discover hope. It comes with the ticket.

Who helped you discover hope?
In what ways do you help others discover hope?

God of hope, I thank you for abundantly meeting my needs. Today teach me Christian financial responsibility. I pray through the name of Jesus. Amen.

Tuesday, Fifth Week of Lent

First things first

But whenever you pray, go into your room and shut the door and pray to your Father who is in secret; and your Father who sees in secret will reward you.
—MATTHEW 6:6

My ninth grade algebra teacher was a classic stern, old-fashioned, dedicated teacher—the toughest I ever had. She insisted that we do algebra just as she taught it. Even if we didn't understand, she was convinced that if we worked through the problem exactly as she taught it, we would understand. She was right. She taught me math.

So it is in our Christian walk. We too often fail to comprehend or understand the complexities of life in times of difficulty and anxiety, but remembering the lessons of Jesus and striving to attain his discipline bring a sense of harmony and order to our confusion and chaos.

It seems to me there is a prerequisite. First things first. Christ Jesus is to prevail in all of life's ventures. God's love is to saturate every fiber of our heart, mind, soul, and strength. It has a beginning, a starting place.

Make that initial commitment. Then, after you have begun your journey, follow up with a secret place of prayer. Jesus wants to communicate with us. Prayer is communication with God. It is listening for God's presence with spiritual ears. It is speaking to Christ as not only our Savior, but our best friend. The Holy Spirit teaches us about prayer, for we do not know how to pray.

Do you have a secret place of prayer?
Is Christ Jesus at home in your heart?

Eternal God, thank you for the gift of prayer. Bless my prayer time today. Let me hear you say that you love me. I pray through the name of Jesus. Amen.

Wednesday, Fifth Week of Lent

The village

*Jesus, looking at him, loved him and said,
"You lack one thing; go, sell what you own,
and give the money to the poor, and you will have
treasure in heaven; then come, follow me."*

—Mark 10:21

Once upon a time there was a village in which some of the people ate lots of apples, hamburgers, pizza, candy, and any food they wanted. Other people had little to eat, only contaminated water to drink, and were very hungry. In that same village some of the children rode buses to school and learned to read and write. Others stood on street corners in dirty clothes, shined shoes, or worked in dark, sweaty places. Some of the people wore name-brand clothes, played video games, attended great sport contests, and had amusement parks for entertainment. Others had nothing to wear, played with toys made from sticks and pieces of plastic, and suffered from sickness and disease. The people who ate the good food, attended the schools, and wore fine clothes lived in nice, comfortable homes. Those who had no food or clothes or schools lived in crowded places or had no homes at all.

One day a father and his son came to visit the village. They saw the rich people and the poor people. As they were leaving the son asked the father, "Why are some of the people so rich and other people so poor?" The father didn't know and just shook his head. The son asked again, "Why don't the rich people, who have warm and comfortable homes, help those who have none?"

The father looked back at the village and shook his head again. He was silent for he had no answer. The name of the village was "Earth."

To inherit the treasure called heaven, we are to provide from our abundance for the people who have no food, schools, medicine, or homes in the village called Earth.

What can you do to help the poor?
How does your giving make a difference to God, to you?

Our heavenly Father, I praise you for the gift of life. I pray that you will bless my offerings to make a difference for others. I pray through the name of Jesus. Amen.

Thursday, Fifth Week of Lent

Peach trees

Let your gentleness be known to everyone. The Lord is near.

—PHILIPPIANS 4:5

Watching an old man dig six holes in the ground was too much for his next door neighbor. "What on earth are you doing?" the inquisitive man asked.

"Planting peach trees," was the matter-of-fact reply of the eighty-year-old neighbor, as he kept digging away.

"But you'll never eat peaches from those trees," the neighbor said.

"No, at my age I know I won't," the elderly man quietly replied. "All my life, I've enjoyed peaches, but never from a tree I planted myself. I wouldn't be eating peaches today if others hadn't done what I'm doing now."

What are we doing to assure that future generations benefit from the blessings that we have received? Others have taught our Sunday School lessons. Others before us have sacrificed to build churches and provide nice places for our worship. Volunteers encouraged us to join the church and to serve in community food kitchens.

Our mission ministries will be decisive factors in providing spiritual nurturing for children being born today. Future generations depend on us. The seeds of faith we plant will affect future generations.

What ministries are you engaged in that will benefit your children or grandchildren?
How will future generations measure your effectiveness in faith-seed planting?

Eternal God, thank you for providing those whose gifts have taught me lessons of faith. Increase my faith that I may be a blessing for future generations of Christians. I pray through the name of Jesus. Amen.

Friday, Fifth Week of Lent

The widow and the teenager

*Truly I tell you, this poor widow has put in more than all those who are contributing to the treasury.
For all of them have contributed out of their abundance; but she out of her poverty has put in everything she had, all she had to live on.*

—MARK 12:43B-44

The small church stood at a country crossroads surrounded by cow pastures. We were singing the hymn that preceded the offertory when a woman shuffled in late and sat at the end of a rear pew. She wore a sagging skirt and a sweater with several missing buttons. Someone said that her husband had died last year and left her penniless.

She pulled a folded handkerchief from her pocket. She unwound the frayed cloth until a crinkled dollar bill appeared. The biblical account of the poor widow who dropped her last meager coins into the temple treasury immediately came to my mind.

As the usher passed the offering plate, the widow passed it on, minus her crinkled dollar. Then she slipped out of the pew and walked quietly across the aisle to a young teenaged girl. If anyone in the church looked more tattered than the poor widow, it was this girl. The widow took the girl's hand, squeezed it, and returned to her pew.

As the offering plate came to rest in the girl's hand, she laid the crinkled dollar in it.

This was no ordinary sacrifice. This widow had given someone else, even poorer than herself, the joy of giving. It's good for us to experience the joy of giving, but doubly good when our giving enables another to experience the joy of giving as well.

When have you seen someone give beyond his or her ability? Think of a way you can give while also enabling another to give.

O Lord my God, thank you for the gifts of life, love, and abundance. Create in me a joyful, giving spirit. I pray through the name of Jesus, my Lord. Amen.

Saturday, Fifth Week of Lent

Mysteries

…looking to Jesus the pioneer and perfecter of our faith, who for the sake of the joy that was set before him endured the cross, disregarding its shame, and has taken his seat at the right hand of the throne of God.

—Hebrews 12:2

A small boy asked his mother, "Mom, who made God?"

The answer is mysterious. God has always been. This truth is beyond the comprehension of our finite minds because our understanding grasps for the origin of things.

We know about birth. We know about the glaciers creating hills and lakes. But who made God?

Easter is another mystery—Jesus resurrected from the grave. The why of Easter is known only in the realm of faith. Although faith is also a mystery, it stems from all creation hoping for good. As we hope for good, we learn that God is good. God's goodness includes an eternal plan. When this eternal plan is accepted, even if it is not understood, our souls respond with joy and exhilaration. The mystery of Easter creates hope in us.

Repentance and the change that comes about in us are also mysteries. Alfred Nobel invented dynamite. When his brother died, the Stockholm newspaper mistakenly printed Alfred's obituary instead. It described a man whose invention would bring destruction and death to thousands. He decided to change his legacy. With his fortune, he endowed the Nobel Foundation, which yearly awards the Nobel Peace Prize to an individual whose work leads to peace and not war.

The people of Jesus' day understood the purpose of crosses. They were instruments of torture. Jesus' call to the disciples included taking up their cross every day (Luke 9:23). It was not a very cheerful approach to ministry. Those who remained faithful paid an enormous price. They were ridiculed; they lost families, fortunes, and some lost their lives. Yet the world was changed and the good news of God in Christ Jesus has never ceased being proclaimed.

The call for us has not changed. It means sacrifice. It includes carrying the cross. The cross of Jesus was an intentional decision to suffer for the benefit of the whole world. The response to Christ in mission brings great benefits to millions of people every day.

As we approach Holy Week and Easter Day, listen for the messages from Christ Jesus concerning truth, love, repentance, forgiveness, giving, and serving.

What mysteries have you experienced?
What blessings are occurring in your life because of Christ's suffering?

O God of truth, thank you for the gift of grace. Today increase my faith that I may attain a heart of love. I pray in the name of Jesus. Amen.

Palm Sunday

A pile of sticks

*I prophesied as he commanded me,
and the breath came into them,
and they lived, and stood on their feet,
a vast multitude.*

—Ezekiel 37:10

I was visiting with Mr. Post. He was in his back yard maintaining some fruit trees. He stopped working to chat with me. As we were talking, I noticed a pile of sticks on the ground nearby. The Posts had several trees around their home. I supposed the sticks were branches that had fallen from the trees and Mr. Post was preparing them for disposal. I nonchalantly gathered up the sticks to carry them to a trash bin.

Mr. Post, a kind grandfatherly type, asked me to please not take away the sticks. I immediately put them back, supposing that they would be used for picnicking or perhaps a campfire. He told me that the sticks were for grafting. He was preparing to graft the sticks into the branches of his fruit trees. I had heard of the procedure but had never met anyone who had actually done it. These looked like ordinary, useless sticks to me, but they were much more than that to Mr. Post.

Mr. Post's pile of sticks has become a symbol of hope for me. The Lenten season began with ashes and is moving toward the hope of resurrection. From ashes to hope. It's a reminder that things are not always as they appear. The butterfly emerges from a cocoon. The dragonfly comes from a water beetle. That which appeared useless, lifeless, and without value held potential I could not imagine.

Like the dry, bleached bones in Ezekiel's story, God raised up a great nation of Judah from total defeat. Through the same creative power, God would bring forth apples from what appeared to be dead tree limbs in Mr. Post's backyard. In that same vein, God is changing us. From the ashes of Ash Wednesday, through Lenten spiritual disciplines, and now to Palm Sunday, we are receiving a spiritual awakening. God is preparing us to become greater, more fruitful servants than ever before.

What images and symbols bring hope to you?
When have you seen the ordinary become the extravagant?

O Lord my God, thank you for images of hope. Today I pray to sense your calling to a specific ministry. I pray through the name of Jesus, my Lord and Savior. Amen.

Monday in Holy Week

The boy and the plow

*Let love be genuine; hate what is evil,
hold fast to what is good;
love one another with mutual affection;
outdo one another in showing honor.*

—ROMANS 12:9-10

Bishop Ray Chamberlain tells this story in his *Seasons of Sacrifice*.

A couple, visiting in Korea, saw a father and his son working in a rice paddy. The old man guided the heavy plow as the boy pulled it. "I guess they must be poor," the man said to the missionary, who was the couple's guide and interpreter.

"Yes," replied the missionary. "That's the family of Chi Nevi. When the church was built, they were eager to give something to it, but they had no money. So they sold their ox and gave the money to the church. This spring they are pulling the plow themselves."

After a long silence, the woman said, "That was a real sacrifice."

The missionary responded, "They do not call it a sacrifice. They are just thankful they had an ox to sell."

It all began with God. God gave Jesus, offering himself in human form. The grace of God incarnate in Jesus seizes us. God sacrificing himself gets our attention. It is costly yet exhilarating. Our expressions of giving are reflections of what God did in Jesus.

Our giving begins across the street and spreads across the world. Like the family in Korea, we don't call our giving a sacrifice. We rejoice that we can make an offering.

Are your giving practices reflections of what God did in Jesus?

Loving, holy God, thank you for providing for me in abundance. Guide my Lenten preparations that my life will reflect new life in Christ Jesus. I ask my prayer in the name of Jesus. Amen.

Tuesday in Holy Week

Passions and needs

You do well if you really fulfill the royal law according to the scripture, "You shall love your neighbor as yourself."

—JAMES 2:8

Sometimes I make the bed. Sometimes Karen and I make the bed together. Most of the time Karen makes the bed. When I make the bed there are bumps or wrinkles or something isn't even. The pillows never match.

Even if I never make the bed right, I'm thankful for it. I'm thankful that we don't sleep on a dirt floor with ragged blankets and quilts or on straw in a hut. I'm thankful we have a comfortable house with a bedroom and don't have to huddle and sleep on the city streets, as do thousands of homeless people.

I'm sure we're all equally important to God. I don't know why millions of God's people live in poverty while others have such splendor and abundance. I know that God doesn't will it to be so, yet the world is so bitterly unfair.

I feel bad complaining about bumps, wrinkles, and sheets that aren't even. People in developing nations would be thankful to have only a portion of those things about which I complain.

I'm thankful for the gift of life and the love of God in Christ Jesus. I know I shouldn't complain about insignificant things. The lesson in today's scripture passage makes my feeble attempts at confession seem somehow inadequate.

Frederick Buechner believes that the intersection of our deepest passions and the world's needs indicates our calling. He explains that the calling may change as the world's needs or our deepest passions change.

Where do your deepest passions and the world's needs intersect?
Are you responding to your calling?

My heavenly Father, I thank you for grace. Today I pray that your calling may become clearer to me. I ask this in the name of Jesus, my Lord. Amen.

Wednesday in Holy Week

Older Zacchaeus

*Then Jesus said to him,
"Today salvation has come to this house."*
—Luke 19:9

Those of you who cherish Bible stories will like this story about Zacchaeus, the small, insignificant tax collector who climbed a tree so he could see Jesus. As a result, Jesus went to Zacchaeus's house, restored his self-respect, and announced that salvation had come to his house.

Legend has it that when Zacchaeus was an old man he still dwelt in Jericho. Every morning at sunrise he went out for a walk and came back with a calm, happy composure, regardless of his mood when he left. After his walk he was ready to begin his day's work with kindness and joy.

His wife wondered where he went on those walks, but he never spoke to her about the matter. So being curious, she followed him one morning.

He went straight to the tree from which he had first seen Jesus. Taking a large urn to a nearby spring, he filled it with water, carried it to the tree, and poured it around the roots. He pulled up all the weeds around the tree. Then he looked up among the branches where he'd sat that day when he met Jesus. A new light of peace and contentment came into his eyes. He turned away with a smile of gratitude and returned ready to do his daily work.

Zacchaeus knew the importance of keeping the spirit of that unusual experience alive, and to do so he tried to keep the tree alive. So it is with us. We never forget the difference God has made in our lives through the gift of salvation in Christ Jesus.

Have you had a conversion experience?
How are you keeping your faith up to date?

Holy God, today I thank you for the gift of redemption. May my life be a blessing to others today because of your forgiveness. I pray through the name of Christ Jesus. Amen.

Maundy Thursday

Maggie and Juan

By this everyone will know that you are my disciples, if you have love for one another.

—John 13:35

From somewhere comes this story:

"This won't be easy," I told Maggie as we approached the crumbling house in the ghetto. We stood on the rotten steps in our prim public health blue uniforms, clutching nurses' black bags. We had come to see Juan. He was seven, a reluctant little boy desperately in need of immunizations. On my previous visit he had refused to let me touch him, so this time I brought Maggie. She had been visiting crumbling houses and reluctant little boys since before I was born. If anyone could persuade Juan, it was Maggie.

Juan's dark, suspicious eyes peered at us from the doorway. In his dirty little hand was the grimiest bologna sandwich I had ever seen.

"Hello, Juan," Maggie said.

He stared at her glumly and took a bite of that filthy sandwich that looked as if it had been fished out of a mud puddle. The wall was still there, only bigger, and I doubted even Maggie could bring it down.

She knelt beside him and said, "I sure am hungry." Juan gave her an uncertain look. So did I. "I really like bologna," she said. He studied his half-eaten sandwich and slowly, hesitantly held it out to her. She swallowed hard and took a bite. A big bite. With that hard ball of bread and bologna and dirt in her mouth, she looked positively humble. And Juan? He flashed her a smile as big as the Rio Grande. Then he held out his arm and became immune to some pretty terrible diseases.

Maggie knew that the best way to reach someone on the other side of an invisible wall is to stoop under it. Try humbling yourself. It's as easy—and as hard—as biting a dirty bologna sandwich.

How have you humbled yourself to be a blessing to others?

Holy God, thank you for the holy meal you instituted for us. May I sense your holiness in all my meals. I pray in the name of Jesus. Amen.

Good Friday

Six hours

When it was noon, darkness came over the whole land until three in the afternoon.

—MARK 15:33

Darkness covered the earth from noon until 3:00 p.m. on that first Good Friday. Darkness often indicates evil or separation from God. During the dark time on Good Friday, our sins were unloaded onto Jesus. The Son of God became our sacrifice. He did for us what we could not do for ourselves. He took on himself the shame, the punishment, and the suffering that we deserve.

For six hours Jesus hung on the cross, separated from God. I have heard it said that it was for joy that he endured the cross. Whose joy? His? My conclusion is that it was for my joy. Jesus knew that someday, even some 2,000 years into the future, I would need a Savior. Therefore, he endured the cross, for my joy.

I made that soul-wrenching discovery several years ago. I have not been the same since. Have you thought deeply about what Jesus was doing in the crucifixion? When you do, it will change your life. You will never be the same again.

Jesus died to pay a debt he did not owe, because I owed a debt I could not pay.

How has your life changed as a result of the crucifixion? Tell someone about it today.

Holy God, today I thank you for the cross. May my life be a blessing for you today. I ask this in the name of Jesus. Amen.

Holy Saturday

Cold grits

*If any want to become my followers,
let them deny themselves and
take up their cross and follow me.*

—MATTHEW 16:24

Willis Moore recalls that his grandmother always ate cold grits, though she preferred them hot. It was her priorities that caused her to eat them cold. Willis fondly remembers how his grandmother cooked a hot breakfast—fresh farm eggs, crisp bacon, homemade blackberry jelly, biscuits, and bowls of hot grits. The family gathered around the table and his grandfather asked the blessing. Then everyone ate—everyone but Grandmother.

While the family was eating breakfast, Grandmother read devotions to the family. When she prayed, everyone stopped eating and bowed their heads. Afterward, everyone cheerfully joined in table conversation while finishing breakfast. Only then, Willis remembers, did Grandmother start to eat, and that is why she always ate cold grits.

Willis remembers those special mornings and the example of his grandmother. At that time it didn't seem all that important, but as the years rolled on he came to recognize the significance of those cold grits. "Spiritual formation," he writes, "is the memory of Grandmother putting God first at breakfast. Of course she did so in the other areas of her life, too, but the memory of her putting aside a hot breakfast to share God's word with her family feeds me yet."

Today we think of Christ lying lifeless in the cold, dark tomb, after the ultimate act of self-sacrifice for us. Our acts of self-denial are seldom so final or extreme—eating cold grits may be all that is asked of us. But there is grace in even the smallest sacrifice, and a reflection of Jesus's redemptive love everytime we put God first.

How are you practicing self-denial to feed your soul?

Holy God, thank you for the gift of love. Today, help me to be a blessing to others. I offer this prayer in the glorious name of Jesus. Amen.

Easter Day

The Resurrection of the Lord

*While they were perplexed about this,
suddenly two men in dazzling clothes stood beside them.
The women were terrified and bowed their faces
to the ground, but the men said to them,
"Why do you look for the living among the dead?
He is not here, but has risen."*

—Luke 24:4-5

Easter Day! Joyful! Triumphant! Victorious!

One of my favorite Easter stories comes from Cecil B. DeMille, the great movie producer. In a canoe on a Maine lake deep in the woods one summer, he floated idly while working on a movie script. Soon he was in the shallow water bumping the bottom, and he noticed that a water beetle had crawled from the lake bottom, attached itself to the canoe hull, and died.

Thinking no more about it, he returned to the script. But then he heard the shell of the water beetle cracking open, and he looked down to see a dragonfly emerge. Its wings propelled it into flight, covering more space in half a second than a water beetle could crawl in a day. The dragonfly flew above the water and the water beetles down below couldn't see it.

Today we remember the miracle of Easter. Jesus Christ became the sacrifice for our sins, enduring our punishment, that we may have forgiveness of sins. Through the resurrection we catch a glimpse of what God has in store for us.

We may not understand the cycle that takes place in the creation of the dragonfly, but we know the water beetle goes through a radical change. The followers of God in Christ Jesus will also experience a dramatic change.

> *Soar we now where Christ has led,*
> *Alleluia!*
> *Following our exalted Head,*
> *Alleluia!*
> —CHARLES WESLEY

How will your celebration of Easter be a witness for Christ Jesus?

O God, thank you for resurrection hope. Keep my witness strong. I pray through the name of the resurrected Jesus. Amen.

If you enjoyed our Lenten meditations, then consider these other Forward Movement resources…

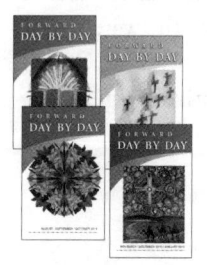

Forward Day by Day

If the meditations in this Lenten book have touched your heart, stirred your soul, or aided your prayer life, we invite you to subscribe to *Forward Day by Day*, which has guided the daily prayer of millions of readers around the world since 1935. Issued quarterly, *Forward Day by Day* brings you an assortment of authors, both clergy and lay and from varied backgrounds, who share their abiding faith in God as they reflect on a Bible passage for the day. *Forward Day by Day* is available in regular or large print, email, Spanish, and Braille, and as a single subscription or a bulk standing order.

Walking With God Day by Day

Inspired by our quarterly *Forward Day by Day*, this book offers 365 meditations bound together— for a year of prayer. Join eleven authors—both new voices and familiar favorites—as they reflect on experiences of finding God in the everyday, sharing wisdom, joy, tears, and laughter as the seasons change and months pass. These meditations are not tied to any particular calendar year, allowing you to begin at any point and follow along for the next twelve months. 384 pages

#2074 — $14.95 (10 or more copies are $10.00 each)

**For more information visit our website
www.forwardmovement.org
or call — 1-800-543-1813**